THE ANTIDOTE

"I have created the yetzer hara, *and I have created Torah as its antidote"* (KIDDUSHIN 30b)

"Truth"—this is Torah
(BERACHOTH 5b)

SHRAGA SILVERSTEIN

THE
ANTIDOTE

SPECIAL OUTREACH EDITION
PUBLISHED BY:

THE KEST-LEBOVITS
JHRL
JEWISH HERITAGE
& ROOTS LIBRARY
A Project of the Foundation for the
Advancement of Torah Study

ISBN 0-87306-173-x
Published 1979
JHRL Non-Profit Edition, 1994

Copyright © 1979 by Shraga Silverstein

All rights reserved, including translation rights.
No part of this publication may be translated
reproduced, stored in a retrieval system or transmitted
in any form or by any means
electronic, mechanical, photocopying, recording or otherwise
without prior permission, in writing, of the copyright owner.

This special non-profit edition has been published
by gracious permission of RABBI SHRAGA SILVERSTEIN
for the sole purpose of making the rich heritage of the Jewish people
more easily available to those who seek it.

Published by:
The Kest-Lebovits
Jewish Heritage and Roots Library
P.O.B. 16068
Bayit-Vegan Station, Jerusalem 91160
Israel

PRINTED IN ISRAEL

לעילוי נשמות הורי שלמה וחי' קעסט שיח'
לוס אנג'לס, קליפורניה

IN MEMORY OF THE PARENTS OF
SOL & CLARA KEST שיח', LOS ANGELES, CALIF.

יצחק אלימלך ב"ר אברהם זאב זצ"ל
חי' פרידא בת ר' שלמה זצ"ל
לבית קעסט, ווילחביץ

צבי ב"ר עזרא הלוי זצ"ל
בתי' בת ר' פסח זצ"ל
לבית אדלער, דיביווע

ת.נ.צ.ב.ה.

לעילוי נשמתם של הרב ברוך בן הרב פסח ליבוביץ זצ"ל

הרבנית לאה בת הרב יהודה ליבוביץ זצ"ל

והבחור ישראל אריה בן הרב ברוך ליבוביץ זצ"ל

ת.נ.צ.ב.ה.

מוסד המוסד לעידוד לימוד התורה

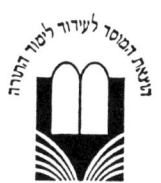

THE FOUNDATION FOR THE ADVANCEMENT OF TORAH STUDY
SPONSORS OF THE LEBOVITS-KEST MEMORIAL
B'NEI-TORAH COMPACT LIBRARY

מוקדש לזכר נשמת

אבי מורי
ר' יוסף ב"ר שרגא הלוי ז"ל
נפטר ז' אייר תשל"ו

ואמי מורתי
ליבא בת ר' שאול הלוי ז"ל
נפטרה ב' אדר ב' תשל"ו

CONTENTS

Foreword · *5*

1 "But You Can't Take the Country Out of Salem" · *9*

2 The *Yetzer Hara* · *12*

3 The Camel · *17*

4 An Application of the Principle · *22*

5 An Earlier Application · *24*

6 The Camel's Hump · *26*

7 An Application of the Principle · *29*

8 The Flaming Lion · *32*

9 The Uninvited · *39*

10 The Man · *52*

11 "If Your Foe is Hungry, Feed Him Bread"· *58*

12 The Beehive · *63*

13 What is *Tzniuth*? · *67*

14 Afterword · *79*

By the same author:

The Path of the Just (transl. Mesillath Yesharim)
The Gates of Repentance (transl. Sha'arey Teshuvah)
Hear, My Son
To Turn the Many to Righteousness
The Knowing Heart (transl. Da'ath Tevunoth)
The Essential Torah Temimah
The Book of Mitzvoth (Maimonides)
The Book of Middos
A Candle by Day

FOREWORD

It was years ago that I read in (the long defunct, lately exhumed) *Life* magazine of a poll among (I forget just how many) American males, purportedly establishing that a certain response, once regarded as lewd, was actually instinctive — with the inevitable conclusion, of course, that it should, therefore, be divested of its conventional opprobrium. I was struck then (as I continue to be struck now by the even more frequent and more glaring recurrences of the same phenomenon) at how deftly the mass media can convert to "nature" what the Torah forbids.

The Torah does not legislate against nature. Correctly understood, and in its highest sense, Torah is nature's manual. How can the polls, then, seem to indicate otherwise? Of course, the polls might be in error; but it is not even necessary to resort to this possibility. The truth is that two ancient confusions lie at the root of the paradox: 1) the confusion of normalcy with nature; 2) the confusion of second-nature with nature. The fact that "everybody is doing it" (whatever "it" is) is no indication that "it" *must* be done; and the fact that something is "natural" does not necessarily mean that it was always so, or that it must always be so. That all-pervasive principle of human behavior *hergeil na'aseh teva* ("Habit becomes nature") was axiomatic to our great men in all generations. The problem is that it is not that evident to *us*, so that something need only be described as "natural" or "instinctive" for many of us to unthinkingly assume that all of mankind is perforce subsumed within the province of these labels.

The result is all too obvious. The media have so subtly exercised their invidious, corrosive influence that a large segment of the Torah community have assimilated the value system of a culture antagonistic to Torah. And they have done so, either entirely unaware that this assimilation has occurred at all, or assuming that what has occurred is not the assimilation of a culture, but the affirmation of human nature!

In no area has the havoc thus wrought been greater than in that of human sexuality. The extent of ignorance, misapprehension, and susceptibility to media manipulation among Torah Jews in this area absolutely beggars description. We have been fed a picture of ourselves and have swallowed it lock, stock, and barrel, not even recognizing that it *is* only a picture — and not one of reality at that! Romance has become the *summum bonum* of many of our co-religionists, and our vision of a Torah life has become strangely interlarded (the metaphor is intentional) with elements that were never intended to form a part of it. The ghastly paradox is that when many of us assume we are at our closest approach to Torah, we are actually at its farthest remove — in far greater proximity to Madison Avenue than to Sinai!

The moral is clear. "Life" in *Life* magazine is to be understood as signifying not what life *is*, in essence, but what it has *become*; and what life has become is as defunct as *Life* magazine and its more brazen mass-medial cohorts of the present day. The only way out of the morass for the sincere, thinking Jew is to rediscover himself in the light of Torah, to get himself to see as culture what others would have him see as nature, to consciously re-inject himself into the perceptual mainstream of Torah, to see with Torah's eyes and to feel with Torah's heart — in short, to derive his self-image not from *Life* (in both senses) but from Torah.

What I wrote in my "Translator's Preface" to *Mesillath Yesharim* applies with special cogency in the highly sensitive and terribly confused area of human sexuality: "If we are to be taught how to know, we must be taught what we are, what we can and cannot expect of ourselves, and what we may reasonably demand of ourselves. Self-knowledge is the very pivot on which *Mesillath Yesharim* turns; and it is in laying bare to us the possibilities and limitations, the subtle by-ways and shadowy recesses of our minds and hearts that *Mesillath Yesharim* has performed for us perhaps its most invaluable service."

It is to works like *Mesillath Yesharim* that we should go for an understanding of what we, life, and nature truly are. I would hope that what follows is written in the spirit of that great work and will contribute in some measure towards that exalted realization of the *Godly* nature implanted within us — *mamlecheth kohanim vegoy kadosh* ("a kingdom of priests and a holy nation").*

---

* It should be borne in mind by the reader that the present work, as the title implies, is confined to the "antidote" area of human sexuality, and does not deal with the far broader area of the sanctity of the Jewish marital union.

1 / "BUT YOU CAN'T TAKE THE COUNTRY OUT OF SALEM"*

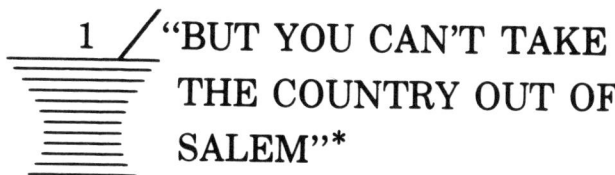

And why not? Why are the verdant meadows, the limpid streams, and — we might add — the sun-drenched lovers, so intimately enmeshed with the tissue paper and tobacco leaf that dangle from their lips that, try as we might (if it ever occurred to us to try), we simply cannot free ourselves of the notion that tissue and leaf are not tissue and leaf at all, but, somehow, the very essence of meadow, stream, and love itself? Indeed, why *can't* we take the country out of Salem?

And why can't we take the courage, strength, and determination — indeed, all of the manly virtues — out of the prognathous jaw of the Marlboro man, who sits

* (Advertisement for Salem cigarettes)

atop his Marlboro steed, overlooking the grand, rugged reaches of Marlboro Country? One, if she were so inclined, might even wed herself to those manly virtues, only to awake one morning to the horrendous realization that she had married — a jaw!

"A stone. Another stone. Man passes and sees the two lying side by side. But what does this stone know of the one beside it? Or what does the water know of the drain in which it flows? Man sees the water and the drain; he sees the water running into the drain, and he comes to fancy that the water, as it goes, may be confiding to the drain — who knows what secrets?

"Ah, what a starry night over the roofs of this little mountain hamlet! Looking up at the sky from these roofs, one would swear that those brightly shining orbs beheld nothing else.

"Yet the stars do not even know there is an earth.

"Those mountains. Is it possible that they are not aware of this little hamlet which has nestled between them since time immemorial? Their names are known: Monte Corno; Monte Moro; and yet, can it be, they do not even know they are mountains? And is it possible that that house over there, the oldest in the village, does not know that it came to be there on account of the road that runs by it, which is the oldest of all roads? Can it, really, be?

"And supposing that it *is* so?

"Go ahead and believe, then, if you like, that the

* 11 * *the country out of Salem*

stars see nothing but the roofs of your little mountain hamlet . . . "*

For if you *do* believe such things — or marry the Marlboro jaw — or fail to take the country out of Salem — you will hardly be the first to have been made the dupe of . . .

---

* From *The Cat, A Goldfinch, and the Stars,* by Luigi Pirandello.

2 / THE YETZER HARA

In the second chapter of *Moreh Nevuchim*, Rambam speaks of a question propounded to him by an "objector." The question runs substantially thus: Is it conceivable that God should reward one for disobedience? What greater disobedience is there than man's eating from the Tree of Knowledge in open defiance of God's command — and what greater reward than the ability to discriminate between good and evil? Man rebels against his Maker and is "punished" with the acquisition of his noblest faculty!

This, in essence, is Rambam's answer: Upon analysis it will be found that man was not rewarded, but, indeed, punished. The nature of this punishment will become evident by a comparison of man's state before the sin with his state thereafter.

✷ 13 ✷ the yetzer hara

(*Genesis* 1:27): "And God created man in His form": God has no corporeal form. The word "form" *(tzelem)* is used here in its figurative sense, as signifying the essential quality of a thing. God's essential quality is truth. [(*Yoma* 69b): "The seal (or trademark) of the Holy One blessed be He is truth."] The meaning of the verse, then, is that Adam was created with the same *type* (not degree) of perception as that possessed by the Holy One blessed be He, Himself. He was created with an intellect which could distinguish *truth* from *falsity*. When he defied God's command and ate from the Tree of Knowledge, he *fell* from this sublime, Divine state to his present *lowly* condition, where he can no longer distinguish the *true* from the *false,* but *only* (and only if he has not perverted himself) the *good* from the *bad.* Adam was not rewarded; he was sorely punished.*

---

* It should be noted that this formulation is not peculiar to Rambam. He himself draws our attention to the fact that, in his translation of *Genesis* 3:5: "For *Elokim* [God] knows that on the day that you eat from it your eyes will be opened and you will be like *elohim*, knowing good and evil" — Onkelos (who received the tradition from the Sages) renders the second *elohim* as *ravrevin* ("great ones"). [It is used in this sense several times in Scripture.] The first *Elokim* Onkelos translates conventionally as "God." Why this strange dichotomy? Onkelos had received it by tradition that God knows not good and evil, but true and false. Of course, it remains to be explained why Adam and Eve would thus be rendered "great ones," but that is not our present purpose.

Again, the verse (*Genesis* 3:22) that we unthinkingly translate as: "And the Lord God said: Behold, the man has become as one of us [God and the angels], knowing good and evil," Onkelos translates: "And the Lord God said: Behold, man has become unique in the world from it [the Tree of Knowledge], to know good and evil." It should be obvious why Onkelos avoids the obvious.

What is the nature of this punishment? Why should the perception of good and evil be a curse relative to the perception of truth and falsity? Here some explanation is necessary.

To say that we see something as true is to say that we see it virtually mathematically. Two and two is four. This is "true"; it is not "good." Two and two is seventeen. This is "false"; it is not "bad." In the realm of the true and the false, there is crystal clarity and universal agreement. Two and two will be four to the vicar of virtue and the viceroy of vice alike. In the realm of the good and the evil, however, this is not the case. What might strike me as good, might strike you as evil. This not to say that there *should* not be one good and evil for all of us. There *should* — but there *isn't!*

A hypothetical example might help. If we saw one man pursuing another with a knife, most of us might shout (in a philosophical sense, of course):"Stop! What

---

And it should not be surprising to us now why that greatest of "plain-meaning" expositors, Rashi himself, follows Onkelos's lead and embarks upon one of his most uncharacteristically circuitous renderings: "*He* is unique among the terrestrial creations as *I* am unique among the celestial ones [though the angels also possess a true-false intellect, God possesses it to its highest *degree*]. And what is *his* uniqueness? — to know good and evil, which is not the case with beasts and animals." [When man possessed a true-false intellect, he was considered one of the celestial creatures — but he was not then unique.]

It should be clear, then, that Rambam is not unique in his interpretation.

you are about to do is *evil!*" The New Guinea headhunter (assuming he were the pursuer and not the pursued) would see our "evil" as "natural," or "necessary," or "good" — or even "godly"! If Adam had witnessed such a sight in Eden *before* he had eaten from the Tree of Knowledge (of course, he couldn't have), what might have issued from his true-false monitor might have been some such expostulation as: "Stop! What you are about to do is *false!* It is absurd! It is unheard of! It is inconceivable! It is as ridiculous as two and two is seventeen!"

The point, I think, is sufficiently clear. In the world of true and false, the truth is transparent. There are no moral dilemmas. Things are seen as they should be seen — indeed, as God Himself sees them. The world of good and evil, on the other hand, is a world of clouded vision, where only the blurred outlines of things are seen, where sharpness and distinctness are lost, and where it is even possible for our vision to deteriorate to the extent that what we perceive as good is not even truth blurred, but falsity blurred; and what we perceive as evil, not even falsity blurred, but truth blurred. [(*Isaiah* 5:20): "Woe to those who call evil good and good evil; who take darkness for light and light for darkness; who take bitter for sweet, and sweet for bitter!"] The first phase of moral astigmatism is indistinctness; the second is perversion.

But who is the culprit in this universal cataclysm? What monumental force is it that can transform a world of crystal-clear truth and falsity to one of muddled good and evil? We have many names for it, but the Holy One Himself called it *ra* (*Sukka* 51b) — the "*yetzer hara.*"

Just what is the nature of this *yetzer hara*?

3 / THE CAMEL

The first, immediate, repercussion of man's descent from the empyrean heights of true-false to the somber depths of good-evil was the trauma of his nakedness. (*Genesis* 3:7): "And they knew that they were naked." But how can this be? How could Adam and Eve perceive something with the faulty vision of good-evil that they were unable to perceive with the perfect vision of true-false! Why were they not ashamed of their nakedness *before* they tasted from the Tree of Knowledge? The answer: before they ate, they *were* not naked; at most they were uncovered. The trees were not naked, the birds were not naked, their table was not naked, and *they* were not naked. They saw in each other nothing of what is now connoted by the word "nakedness." They saw each other as they *were* —

through the eyes of *truth*. The very fact that Adam and Eve saw new things in each other after eating from the forbidden tree was an indication to them that they had entered a different perceptual world. They knew (from their memory of the truth) that the new things did not belong there. Instead of seeing human tissue as human tissue, they found themselves investing it with all manner of qualities which they "remembered" were not inherent in it. They seemed to be seeing, but they *knew* they were *imagining*. Yet, try as they might to restore their old vision, they could not. They could not (and there is no attempt whatsoever to be facetious here) — they could not "take the country out of Salem." They knew they had fallen from the truth — and they were ashamed! Here, according to Rambam, lies the culprit in the saga of man's shame; the catalyst in the conversion of a true-false to a good-evil universe — IMAGINATION (*dimyon*), imagination operating from the base of man's bodily appetites. This is the *yetzer hara*.

In the second book of *Moreh Nevuchim* (Chapter 30), Rambam recapitulates the dynamics of Adam's fall, beginning with a Midrashic allegory. (The bracketed comments in the discussion that follows are based upon the classical commentaries.)

(*Pirkey d'R. Eliezer* 13): "Samael . . . saw all the creatures that the Holy One had created, and [among them all] he found none so wise in doing evil as the serpent . . . It was as big as a camel; and he [Samael] mounted and rode on it. . . ."

✳ 19 ✳ *the camel*

Thus, it was actually this rider who enticed Eve. Samael is the name generally applied by our Sages to Satan [= *yetzer hara*] ... There is a meaning in this name [*Sama-El*: "blinding God" — obscuring truth], as there is also in the name *nachash* ("serpent"). [*Nachash* connotes imagination. The snake of Eden was certainly a flesh and blood snake, but it, rather than another creature, was chosen as the instrument for man's downfall because of the quality that it typifies. In this regard it is to be noted that the serpent is described (*Genesis* 3:1) as "slyer (*arum*) than all the beasts of the field" and that the first thing Adam and Eve perceived after eating from the Tree of Knowledge is that they were *arum* ("naked"). That is, the "slyness" of imagination (*nachash*) produces the illusion of "nakedness."] In describing how the serpent came to entice Eve, our Sages say (*ibid.*): "Samael [Satan = *yetzer hara*] was riding on it [using the serpent = imagination, as its vehicle] and God [Truth] was laughing at both the camel [overblown imagination (*gamal* — camel — connotes full development)] and its rider" [*Satan*, who seeks to turn men astray (*satah*) through 'camelized' imagination. Is it any wonder that God laughs! What can be more ludicrous to truth than tissue paper being taken for the country, or human tissue for Paradise!]

It is especially of importance to notice that the serpent did not approach or address Adam [symbolically, the cognitive faculty, man's closest approach to truth], but all his attempts were directed against Eve [symbolically, the appetitive faculty, that area of the human psyche most vulnerable to the wiles of imagination (caution: women's libbers, keep your cool; this has nothing to do with your cause)], and it was through her that the serpent caused injury and death to Adam. The greatest hatred exists between the serpent and Eve [imagination is the body's greatest enemy] and between his seed and her seed; her seed being, undoubtedly, also the seed of man [so that, ultimately, imagination undermines even the cognitive faculty]. More remarkable, still, is the way in which the serpent is joined to Eve (*Genesis* 3:15), or rather his seed to her seed; the head of the one [the serpent] touches the heel of the other [man]. Eve defeats the serpent by crushing its head [the contriver of imaginative wiles], while the serpent defeats her by wounding her heel [that which is at the greatest remove from her head — or cognitive faculty]. This is likewise clear.

The following is also a remarkable passage, most bizarre in its literal sense; but as an allegory it contains wonderful wisdom, and fully agrees with real facts, as those who understand all the chapters of this treatise (*Moreh Nevuchim*) will realize: "When the serpent came to Eve, he infected her with *zuhama* [the poison of imagination]; the Israelites, who stood at Mount Sinai [and received Torah = Truth (see the epigraphs on the title page)] removed that poison [Truth is the antidote to imagination]. Idolaters, who did not stand at Mount Sinai, have not got rid of it . . ." Again: "God

* 21 * *the camel*

[Truth] has never shown the Tree of Knowledge [of good and evil] to man, nor will He [Truth] ever show it" [for it is not truth, but *imagination*, which shows good and evil!]

4 / AN APPLICATION OF THE PRINCIPLE

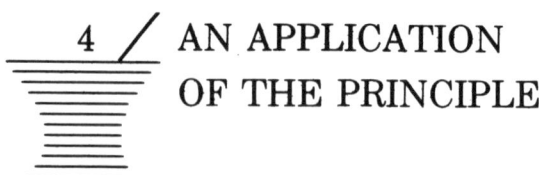

(*Avoda Zara* 17a): R. Chanina and R. Yochanan were once walking along the road, when it diverged into two paths, upon one of which was situated a house of idolatry, and upon the other, a house of prostitution. One said to the other: "Let us take the road which passes by the house of idolatry, the *yetzer hara* for which has been slaughtered" [see "The Flaming Lion," pages 32-38]. The other replied: "Let us rather take the road which passes by the house of prostitution, so that we can subdue our *yetzer hara* and be rewarded for it." [The latter course was followed.] When they got there, they saw the harlots retreating before them, at which the first asked the second: "How did you know this?" [i.e. What made you so confident that your *yetzer hara* would not get the better of you?] The latter

* 23 * *application of the principle*

replied: "It is written (*Proverbs* 2:11): 'It [Torah *lishma* (studied for its own sake)] will protect you from *zima*' [similar to *zuhama* (see above)]. Understanding [Torah] will guard you."

Caution: Do not assume that you are learning Torah *lishma*.

Consolation: To the extent that your learning *approaches lishma*, to that *extent*, Torah will guard you from *zima*.

5 / AN EARLIER APPLICATION

We are taught (in *Sota* 32b) that Joseph was at the point of yielding to the wife of Potiphar (*Genesis* 39), when the image of his father, Jacob, appeared to him in the window and, at the very last moment, turned him from the act. And for this Joseph has gained our everlasting admiration. But why? Would not anyone, struck by the image of such a father, do the same? The answer lies in another comment on the same episode (*Sanhedrin* 19b): "(*Proverbs* 31:30): 'Favor is false' — this is Joseph." That is, Joseph was victorious in his trial because at the last moment he was able to look squarely at the temptress's Salem Country and say: "You are false! You are nothing but tissue paper and tobacco leaf! Is *this* what I am pursuing!" And, of course, at that point, there was nothing to pursue. As

an earlier application

the *Gemara* tells us (*Sota* 43a), it was not necessary for Joseph to *suppress* his *yetzer hara*, but "*pitpet beyitzro*" — he *ridiculed* his *yetzer hara*, attaching to it no significance whatsoever [see Rashi]. But for the almost superhuman strength of will which must have been necessary to muster up at the last moment the power of truth that could ridicule a *yetzer hara* into oblivion — for this, Joseph certainly deserves, and has received, our unbounded admiration. Joseph was not bludgeoned into submission by the image of his father Jacob. Rather, he steeled himself to rise to what that image represented — Truth! (*Micha* 7:20): "You will give *truth* to Jacob." "The image of Jacob is inscribed under the Throne of Glory" (i.e. Jacob is the human exemplar of God's essential quality — "The seal of the Holy One blessed be He is *truth*").

(*Berachoth* 20a): R. Yochanan would pass by and sit at the door of the ritualarium, saying, "When the daughters of Israel rise from their immersion, let them gaze at me, so that they will have children as beautiful as I." At this, the Rabbis said to him, "But is the master not afraid of the evil eye?" He answered, "I descend from the seed of Joseph, over which the evil eye has no power, as it is written (*Genesis* 49:22): 'Joseph is a son of favor, a son of favor *alei ayin*,' concerning which R. Avahu said: Read it not *alei ayin* ('*on* the eye'), but *oley ayin* ['*above* the eye' — immune to the eye through the power of truth!]"

6 / THE CAMEL'S HUMP

In his treatise, *Morality and Religion*, the French philosopher, Henri Bergson, analyzes the (relatively modern!) phenomenon of romance as an extension of the error of imagination. That is, whereas imagination looks at a thing, and sees a quality *in* it, romance prefabricates a quality (sublimity, for example), looks for a thing to plaster it onto, and, unfortunately, finds it! It may be helpful, for our purposes, to closely scrutinize his formulation: (Again, the bracketed comments are my own.)

"[Emotional] feelings akin to [physical] sensations, closely bound up with the objects which give rise to them, are, indeed, just as likely to attract a previously created emotion [sublimity, for example] as they are to connect with an entirely new one [new, in the sense

* 27 * *the camel's hump*

that the viewer did not have it in his head before he looked at the object — the heroism in the Marlboro jaw, for example]. This is what happened with love. From time immemorial woman must have inspired man with an [ideational, quality-manufacturing] inclination distinct from [physical] desire, but in immediate contact, as though welded to it [as the quality of gentleness of heart, let us say, is 'camel'-wise, welded to soft, smooth, milky-white skin, or as the country is welded to Salem], and pertaining both to [emotional] feeling and to [physical] sensation. But romantic love has a definite date: it sprang up during the Middle Ages on the day when some person or persons [who wanted to have his cake (in the after-life) and eat it (in this life)] conceived the idea of absorbing love into a kind of supernatural feeling, into religious emotion as created by Christianity and launched by the new religion into the world. When critics reproach mysticism with expressing itself in the same terms as passionate love, they forget that it was love which began by plagiarizing mysticism, borrowing from its fervor, its raptures, its ecstasies: in using the language of a passion it had transfigured ['I adore you!' 'I cherish you!' 'Angel, I idolize you!'], mysticism has only resumed possession of its own. We may add that the nearer love is to adoration, the greater the disproportion between the emotion [adoration] and the object [Flossie], the deeper, therefore, the disappointment to which the lover is exposed [when he really gets to know Flossie] — unless he decides that he will ever look at the object through the mist of emotion and never touch it, that he will, in a word, treat it religiously. Note that the ancients had already spoken of the illusions of love, but these were errors akin to those of the senses [i.e. produced *by* observation and not *before* observation], and they concerned [erroneous qualitative conclusions from] the face of the beloved ['She must have the heart of a Mona Lisa'], her figure ['Everything she does is so exquisitely proportioned'], her bearing ['She is majestically statuesque'], her character ['Her speech is the softness of sympathy']. Think of Lucretius's description: the illusion here applies only to the [perceptually generated] qualities of the loved one, and not, as with the modern illusion, to what we can expect of love [by what we bring to it *before* observation]. Between the old [spontaneous] illusion and the illusion we have superadded to it there is the same difference as between the primitive feeling, emanating from the object itself, and the religious emotion summoned from without by which it has been pervaded and eventually submerged. The margin left for disappointment is now enormous, for it is the gap between the divine [God] and [*lehavdil*] the human [Flossie]."

Is there any doubt that modern man has added a hump to the camel?

7 / AN APPLICATION OF THE PRINCIPLE

In commenting upon the verse (*Deuteronomy* 24:1), "If a man takes a woman and lives with her, and it comes to pass that she does not find favor in his eyes, because of some unseemly thing that he has found in her, then let him write her a bill of divorce . . ." Malbim writes:

"This merits consideration. If he has taken her to be his wife and lived with her, then he certainly must have seen her before, and she must have found favor in his eyes — for which reason he married her in the first place! [Whither, then, has her favor fled?] . . . We are hereby provided with a refutation of those scoffers who poke fun at the ways of our fathers, who, when they took wives for their sons, would make inquiry only about the prospective bride's family, the conduct of her father and mother, and her own deportment, and who allowed their sons to look upon the faces of their brides-to-be only before the wedding.

"Consider 'the rock from which we were hewn,' our father Abraham, may peace be upon him. When he wished to take a wife for his one, beloved son, Isaac, his exclusive concern was the maiden's family and homeland. He desired only that she be from his family and from his father's household, whose modesty was known to him. Moreover, he relied entirely in this upon his servant, Eliezer, the doyen of his household, and did not send his son along with him. Then we read (*Genesis* 24:67), 'And Isaac brought her into the tent of his mother, Sarah, and he took Rivka and she became his wife, and [only afterwards] he loved her.'

"Now this was the practice followed by the Jews when they lived in their own land. Their love was like the growth of a tree, which begins from a small seed that the water makes cling to the soil, which grows and expands, more and more, from day to day. So was their love. In the beginning, it was only the seed of love that was planted in the furrows of their hearts; and it was through beauty of deed that this seed grew more and more, from day to day, so that love was at its fullest only *after* marriage. . . .

"And common sense, too, vindicates the custom of our forefathers. For since it was understood by the couple before the wedding that they lacked complete knowledge of each other, there was a tacit agreement between them that even average compatibility would be acceptable. But, under the new mores, the young

* 31 * *application of the principle*

people first become adept at captivating each other, conjuring up between themselves a love which has no basis whatsoever in reality but only in romantic metaphor or theatrical extravaganza. Is it any wonder, then, that when their mutual deception begins to dawn upon them, their 'love' begins to cool off, little by little, until it reaches the point of complete extinction? Is it any wonder, then, that divorce is so much more prevalent today than it was in the past?"

Is it any wonder then?

8 / THE FLAMING LION

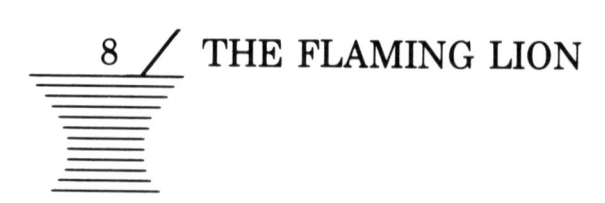

The *Gemara* (*Yoma* 69b) recounts a monumental turning point in the history of the *yetzer hara*, knowledge of which is essential for an understanding of our own natures:

(*Nehemiah* 9:4): "And they cried [during the period of the second Temple] with a great voice to the Lord their God." What did they say? Rav (some say R. Yochanan) said. "Woe! Woe! This [the *yetzer hara* for idolatry] is the culprit that destroyed our [first] Temple, burned our Sanctuary, killed all of the righteous ones, and caused the Jews to be exiled from their land. And it is still 'dancing' among us. Did You not give it to us only so that we would receive reward [by subduing it]? We do not want it, and we do not want its reward."
At this, a shard fell from the heavens, upon which was

33 * the flaming lion

inscribed the word *truth* [i.e. the alternative to the *yetzer hara* (imagination) is truth. (For it is the same imagination which places the country into Salem that places divinity into stones. Hence, the age-old affiliation between idolatry and harlotry, viz. (*Hosea* 4:1): "For my people ask counsel of a piece of wood, and their staff speaks to them; for the spirit of harlotry has led them astray, and they have gone astray lewdly from their God." (*Sanhedrin* 63b): "Israel desired idolatry only to permit itself harlotry"]. (R. Chanina said: It is hereby to be derived that the seal [or trademark] of the Holy One blessed be He is truth.") They sat and fasted for three days and three nights [for the *yetzer hara* to be "handed over" to them], and it was delivered into their hands, emerging as a flaming lion [in intensity] from the Holy of Holies. [It had insinuated itself into the most sacred areas of their lives!] At this, the prophet [Zechariah] said (*Zechariah* 5:8): "This is the wicked one!" As they seized it, a hair tore from its mane, at which it emitted a roar that traveled four hundred parasangs. At this, they said: "What can we do with it? Perhaps it is favored by Heaven!" [The tremendous roar upon the extraction of a hair had served notice upon them that killing it would somehow "roar" the earth out of existence (the "somehow" being that after Adam's eating from the Tree of Knowledge, imagination and body became linked in such a solid bond that to destroy the one — imagination — is to destroy the other — body or matter)]. At this, the prophet said to them:

"Cast it into the leaden cauldron and cover its mouth with lead, so that the roar will be absorbed," as it is written (*ibid.*): "And he cast it into the *eifa*, and he cast the lead cover over its mouth." [I.e. though they could not kill the *yetzer hara*, they were granted a lessening of its intensity (which, however, because of the post-Tree-of-Knowledge bond, made them less intense in *everything*. There's the rub! Our ancestors were giants — in either direction; we are pygmies). This lessening of intensity (symbolized by the absorbing of the roar) sufficed to remove the *yetzer hara* for idolatry. It did not yet suffice to remove that for harlotry. For an imagination that is not intense enough to read a god into a stone is still intense enough to read the country into Salem. The leap is not that great.] Thereupon, they said: "Since it is a time of favor, let us implore Heaven that the *yetzer hara* for lust be handed over to us" [i.e. let us secure a further reduction in intensity sufficient to eliminate *that yetzer hara*]. They prayed, and it was delivered into their hands. At this, the prophet said to them: "Take care, now; if you kill this *yetzer hara* the entire world will be destroyed!" [Being cautious] they had it imprisoned for three days [i.e. they did not kill it, but "unplugged" it, as it were]. During that period they sought a one-day-old egg for a sick person throughout Eretz Yisrael, and they could not find one! [The chickens had stopped laying eggs—*biology* had become unplugged!] At this, they said: "What can we do? If we kill it, the entire world will be destroyed. If we implore

the flaming lion

mercy that it operate by halves [producing only legitimate and not illegitimate desire] — Heaven does not grant halves." Finally, they stained its eyes and set it free [i.e. they could not eliminate it, but they did reduce its intensity] to the extent that [unperverted] men are no longer aroused by their close kin [whereas, previously, incestuous desire had been the norm — thus far, the Talmudic passage].

And this is where we find ourselves now. It remains to be understood, however, why it was only this particular form of desire which was attenuated. To say that Heaven does not operate by halves is to say that it is not arbitrary, that it is consistent in its operations. Gravity pulls us where we would not like to be as well as where we would like to be. And though [moral] individuals certainly like the idea of not being pulled to incest, if they are pulled at all [and they are], then why should they not be pulled there as well?

We are provided with a clue to this question at the end of the first *sidra* of *Genesis* (6:1-2): "And it came to pass, when men began to multiply on the face of the earth and daughters were born to them, that the sons of *elohim* [according to Rambam (*Moreh Nevuchim* I, 14), 'men of a higher order'] saw the daughters of man [again, according to Rambam (*ibid*), 'women of a lower order'] that they were fair, and they took wives of all that they desired." According to Rashi, this connotes an increase in perversion.

The questions are obvious. Were daughters born to men only when they began to multiply on the face of the earth? If the daughters were of a lower order, why should they suddenly seem fair to men of a higher order (who apparently had spurned such women previously) simply because men began to multiply on the face of the earth? And why should the entire process result in an increase in perversion?

Once again, we call Rambam to our aid. The master writes (*Moreh Nevuchim* III, 49): "Another important object in prohibiting prostitution is to restrain excessive and continual lust; for lust increases with the variety of its objects. The sight of that to which a person has been accustomed for a long time does not produce such an ardent desire for its enjoyment as is produced by objects new in form and character." Here, with characteristic terseness, Rambam has stated the principle which resolves our difficulties. Brothers (today) do not desire sisters, and vice versa, because they know each other too well! There is little or no leverage for imagination. Which brother would construe his sister's eyelashes as "the exotic shadows of the Orient"? Merely consider the galaxy of "distance" epigrammatica: "Distance lends enchantment"; "The grass is greener on the other side"; "Absence makes the heart grow fonder"; "the fascination of the unknown"; (conversely, "Familiarity breeds contempt"), etc., etc. The point need not be belabored. The *yetzer hara* is essentially imagination, and as long as you don't know what a thing is, you can imagine it to be anything.

It is not that daughters were born to men only when they began to multiply on the face of the earth, but it was then that these daughters began to pose far more of a "problem" than they had ever posed before. [The usage here corresponds to Rashi's interpretation of *Genesis* 12:11, "Behold, now I know that you are a beautiful woman" — to the effect that it is not that Abraham had never been aware of Sarah's beauty, but that he now saw it as posing a problem.] Because there was now such a relatively great variety of these daughters, and because they were spread over far greater distances, men of a "higher order" (some of the classic expositors of *Moreh Nevuchim* see this as an allusion to the higher faculties) who, in the close quarters of a fledgling civilization, had gotten to know them well enough to spurn them as being of a "lower" order, were suddenly fascinated by their exoticism, and found these same lower-order creatures "fair"! Is it any wonder that such a state of affairs should precipitate an increase of lust and perversion?

No, there are no halves in heaven. It is just that a greater *intensity* of *yetzer hara* is required to invest objects close at hand with exoticism (incest) than to transfigure distant objects in the same manner (conventional lust) — just as a greater *intensity* of *yetzer hara* is required for idolatry than for harlotry. Idolatry demands a flaming lion. A lower flame will suffice for incest, and an even lower one for run-of-the-mill lust.

It is this lowest flame that we are really on today. If, in spite of this, instances of incest and of the other perversions are far from rare in our society, it is not because men are succumbing to (or, as others would have it, "realizing") their natures, but rather, as I have written elsewhere,* because "There are some who go to the Devil without even having been invited."

---

* *Hear My Son*

9 / THE UNINVITED

(*Yoma* 19b): Elijah said to R. Yehuda, the brother of R. Sala Chasida: "You ask why the Messiah has not yet come, when today it is Yom Kippur and many virgins have been violated in Nehardaa!" . . . And what does Satan say to this? "The *satan* is not authorized to entice on Yom Kippur." How do we know this? Rami b. Chamma said: "The *gematria* [numerical equivalent] of 'the *satan*' is 364. All of the other days of the year, he is authorized to entice; on Yom Kippur, he is not authorized to entice."

Well, if he is not authorized to entice, how were they enticed? The answer should be obvious: "There are some who go to the Devil without even having been invited." (Or, to vary the image, if you like, "There are some who fan the lion's flames.")

(*Sukka* 52b): R. Yehuda b. Ilai expounded: In time to come [in the days of the Messiah, when all will recognize the truth and the veil of imagination will be lifted from men's eyes], the Holy One blessed be He will bring the *yetzer hara* and slaughter it before the righteous and before the wicked. To the righteous it will appear as a great mountain; to the wicked it will appear as a strand of hair. The righteous will cry, and the wicked will cry. The righteous will cry [traumatized by the retrospective recognition of the horrible danger they had faced], "How could we have conquered this great mountain!" [They will see how *real* God had made the imaginary seem to them. (*Ibid*): "To the extent that one is greater than his neighbor, to that extent his *yetzer hara* is greater" (otherwise, given his greatness, there would be no free-will contest), and when they see this, they will wonder how they could have overcome it in the first place. And they will recognize that, given *only* the resources of their own free will, they *could* not have overcome it! (*Ibid.*): R. Shimon b. Lakish said: A man's *yetzer hara* intensifies itself over him every day, and desires to kill him, as it is written (*Psalms* 37:32): "The wicked one" — the *yetzer hara* — "eyes the righteous one, and desires to slay him"; and unless the Holy One blessed be He assisted him, he could not overcome him, as it is written (*ibid.* 33): "The Lord will not leave him in his hand." The strength of their will alone would not have been sufficient, but "The Lord assists those who seek purity."] The wicked will cry, "How could we not have

the uninvited

overcome this strand of hair!" [They will be traumatized by the retrospective recognition that they had been confronted with a hair, a will-o'-the-wisp, which should have exercised no power whatsoever over them — if not for the fact that they had wilfully transformed this hair into a mountain — if not for the fact that they had *wanted* to see the country in Salem. The *yetzer hara* had not invited them. They had *chosen* to go!]

And why should they choose to go? Obviously, because it's "easy fun." In discussing the phenomenon of adverse will as the cause of cognitive error (as opposed to the common notion of the second producing the first*), R. Eliyahu Dessler [*Michtav Me'Eliyahu*] adduces the following verse (*Isaiah* 6:9-10): And He said: "Go and tell this people: 'You hear, yet you do not understand; you see, yet you do not know.' The people have made their hearts fat, and their ears heavy, and they have smeared over their eyes, lest they see with

---

* In this regard it is instructive to note that the Torah states (*Numbers* 16:39): "And do not go astray after your heart and after your eyes," as opposed to what we would consider the normal order — eyes seeing and heart desiring. The truth is that we first desire [or imagine] in our hearts, and then see what we want to see — as the mirage-ridden desert nomad is convinced beyond all doubt that he sees an oasis.

It is in the same spirit that we are told (*Pirkey Avoth* 3:27), "If there is no fear of God, there is no wisdom." We wonder why the one should be a prerequisite for the other. But the point is the same. If one has no fear of God, he will structure the universe as he wishes; he will see what he wants to see; and he will fly in the face of the most elementary logic.

their eyes, and hear with their ears, and understand with their hearts, and return and be cured" — upon which Rashi comments: "They forced their hearts not to hear the exhortations of the prophets from fear that they would find reason in their words, and understand in their hearts, and return to Me and be cured"! [They would rather be sick! It's so much more fun seeing Salem Country than tissue paper. (And it really is. The only problem is that seventy-year Salem Country eyes cannot see the eternal, world-to-come God of *Truth.*) With the righteous, then, it is *God* Who has made the mountain out of the mole-hill; with the wicked, it is they themselves who have turned the trick] as it is written (*Zechariah* 8:6): "It [the exposé of the *yetzer hara*] will cause wonder in the eyes of the remnant of these people . . . and it will cause wonder in My eyes too!" [What is it that can cause wonder to God? How can the Author of everything be surprised at anything? There is one thing which (in a sense) God does not author. That is the area of our free will. As the name implies, it is our area of freedom. God "wonders" at the triumph of the righteous. Though He assisted (and we may surmise, quite considerably) in the overturning of the mountain He created, there is an element of that triumph which was produced not by Him, but by the free will of the righteous themselves. God "wonders" at the downfall of the wicked. Their undoing is not attributable to Him, for, after all, why should that strand of hair He created undo them? He has not even assisted in their undoing (for whereas "The Lord *assists* those who seek purity," He only "*leaves the path open* for those who seek impurity"). He has done *none* of it; is it not something for God Himself to "wonder" at?] R. Assi said: "In the beginning, the *yetzer hara* [to the wicked] is like the gossamer thread of a spider-web, and in the end [after imagination has completed its weaving], it is as stout as a cart-rope, as it is written (*Isaiah* 5:18): "Woe to those who draw forth iniquity with cords of deceit [Rashi: In the beginning, they bring it upon themselves (this may be taken in its double sense) with non-existent (purely imaginary) cords] and transgression as with a cart-rope." [It is to be noted (see *Yoma* 36b) that *avon* ("iniquity") connotes *meizid* (intentional sin), whereas *chata'a* ("transgression") connotes *shogeg* (unintentional sin). The usage in this case should be obvious. It is in the first stage, when the sinner allows himself to be "bowled over" by a strand of hair, that the element of *meizid* is most pronounced. Once he has created this mountain, however, it is not surprising that he should be crushed by it; and in this sense (but not in the sense that he is not responsible for having created it in the first place), his sin, at this stage, possesses something of the character of *shogeg*. It should not surprise us either that following almost immediately upon this verse, as the inescapable, inexorable result of this process of hair-weaving, is that haunting, awesome denouement (*ibid.* 20, and see page

15): "Woe to those who call evil good and good evil; who take darkness for light and light for darkness; who take bitter for sweet, and sweet for bitter!"]

Woe to those who draw forth iniquity with cords of deceit! Woe to those "who go to the Devil without even having been invited"!

(*Avoda Zara* 17a): It is told of R. Elazar b. Durdiya that there was not one harlot in the world whom he had not lived with. Once, hearing that there was a harlot in the cities of the sea who demanded a bag of dinars as her fee, he took a bag of dinars and crossed seven seas to get to her ["Distance lends enchantment"]. In the midst of the act, she passed wind, and said: "Just as this wind will not return to its place, so the penance of R. Elazar b. Durdiya will not be accepted."[The spell of exoticism thus traumatically broken], he went and sat between the mountains and the hills and cried, "Mountains and hills, implore mercy for me!" [I.e. Just as you are firmly fixed and all-enduring, so is my desire. It is fixed within me; it is part of the immutable scheme of things; it is Nature!] They answered, "Before we implore mercy for you, we should implore mercy for ourselves, for it is written (*Isaiah* 54:10): 'For the mountains shall depart and the hills shall be removed.'" [I.e. You appeal to us as typifying unassailable nature? We ourselves are assailable! We are not an unalterable natural phenomenon, from which you may draw conclusions as to the unalterability of your own nature and the "naturalness" of your desire.] At this, he cried, "Heaven and earth, implore mercy for me!" [If not the mountains and the hills, then certainly *you* must typify fixed, omnipotent, unchallengeable nature.] They answered, "Before we implore mercy for you, we should implore mercy for ourselves, as it is written (*ibid.* 51:6): 'For the heavens shall vanish away like smoke, and the earth shall rot like a garment.' " At this, he cried, "Sun and moon, implore mercy for me!" They answered, "Before we implore mercy for you, we should implore mercy for ourselves, as it is written (*ibid.* 24:23): 'Then the moon shall be confounded, and the sun ashamed.' " At this, he cried, "Stars and constellations, implore mercy for me!" They answered, "Before we implore mercy for you, we should implore mercy for ourselves, as it is written (*ibid.* 34:4): 'And all the host of heaven shall rot away.' " [In fine, there is no natural phenomenon whatsoever which can serve as a paradigm for the irrefragability of your own nature.] At this, he said "[It is not my nature], it is *me!*" [i.e. my *will*], whereupon he placed his head between his knees and groaned until his soul departed. [I.e. his deception had become so completely ingrained in his being that to break it (as he succeeded in doing at that moment) was to break his very self. Compare the repercussions of killing the universal *yetzer hara*, page 33.] At this, a heavenly voice called out: "R. Elazar b. Durdiya is now readied for life in the world-to-come!" [He is purged of imagination and readied for Truth.]

On this point of the relationship between the capabilities of our natures and the expectations of

Torah, *Meshech Chochma* states: (*Leviticus* 18:1-5): Our Sages have already explained in their works that the Torah did not promulgate commandments which would pose a threat to the union of body and soul, but only such as could be borne by the generality of society and which would promote the natural well-being of all. This is the intent of their dictum that the positive and the negative commandments correspond, respectively, to the 248 organs and 365 sinews of the human body. The Creator made man "just," so that his parts correspond to those of the Torah, thus making it possible for the soul to direct the body along the miraculously ordered path of the Blessed One. The Torah did not enact more dietary restrictions than human nature could bear, and it placed only such restrictions upon conjugal relations as best conduced to the propagation of the species, homeostasis, and the like. . . . Therefore, in these verses ["And the Lord spoke to Moses, saying: Speak to the children of Israel and say to them: I am the Lord your God. As the deeds of the land of Egypt, in which you dwelt, you shall not do; and as the deeds of the land of Canaan, into which I bring you, you shall not do. Neither shall you walk in their statutes. You shall do My judgments and keep My ordinances, to walk in them; I am the Lord your God. You shall keep My statutes and My judgments, which, if a man does, he shall live through them; I am the Lord"] we are told not to imagine that it is difficult or impossible for the body to abide by the laws governing illicit relations. This is the intent of "I am the Lord *your* God," i.e. I am your Creator, and I know your nature and the governing principles of your organism. It is not overly difficult to curb lust and bridle desire, and it is I [your Creator] who command that you not emulate the [licentious] deeds of Egypt and Canaan . . . and that you heed My statutes and My judgments, which, if a man does, he shall live through them — for they are designed to give life to the human organism and to guide it upon such a course as will provide it with the greatest good in the world and with a blessed portion in the world-to-come — and they will not compass its death! And this is the meaning of the Sages' dictum [on "Moses, saying" above], i.e., "Just as the Blessed One commanded me [Moses] to separate completely from my wife, knowing, as He did, that I had refined my material nature to sapphiric fineness, that my flesh had been transmuted to spirit, and that, having been translated beyond the human, carnal compound, I could abide by this command — in the same way, when He commanded you, the children of Israel, in regard to illicit relations, the Omniscient One most assuredly knew that the Torah regimen in this area would best serve body and soul alike, and would be as easily observable as all of the other prohibitions in the Torah."

Indeed, where the Torah knew that restrictions in this area would be unobservable, it did not make such restrictions, so that in the case of *yefath to'ar*, for example [literally "a woman of beautiful form," taken captive in wartime] the Torah, recognizing that "the *yetzer hara* is especially intense in time of danger," permitted her to her captor, though she is otherwise forbidden. As explained in the *Gemara* (*Kiddushin* 22a): "The Torah legislated apropos of the *yetzer hara*. It is better that Jews eat the flesh of a moribund animal that has been ritually slaughtered rather than that of one which has died of itself" — upon which Rashi comments: "The implication is that because her beauty intensely arouses his evil inclination, she was grudgingly permitted to him, it being preferable that Jews eat flesh of an animal that was slaughtered at the point of death, though this be revolting . . . and not eat flesh of an animal that has died of itself and has become *neveilah* [ritually impure]." In other words, as Rashi tersely states on the verse itself, "If the Holy One blessed be He did not permit her, he would marry her unlawfully." Now this is certainly not to be understood as a carte blanche lifting of a prohibition whenever its observance becomes tedious (for such a policy would produce the absurdity of permitting murder if one would kill in any event). It constitutes, rather, a recognition on the part of the Torah of the bounds of human nature, of what can and what cannot be expected of the generality of mankind. If the Torah lifts a prohibition, it is because mankind *cannot* abide by it.

It is in the same spirit that the following is to be understood (*Nedarim* 20a): R. Yochanan b. Dehavai said: "Four things **were** revealed to me by the ministering angels . . . **Some** children are born deaf and dumb because their parents converse during in-

* 49 * the uninvited

tercourse. . . ." This was countered: Did we not learn: Imma Shalom [the wife of R. Eliezer] was asked: "Why are your children so beautiful?" And she answered: "Because he speaks with me neither in the beginning of the night nor in the end of the night [when he might hear the voices of women walking outside and give thought to them], but only in the middle of the night; and when he does speak with me, he uncovers a *tefach* and covers a *tefach* [and hastens through the act] as if a demon were forcing him to it. And I asked him: 'Why is it [that you speak with me only then]?' He answered: 'So that I not give thought to another woman and [in that sense] father illegitimate children.' " [We see, in any event, that he *did* converse with her during intercourse!] There is no contradiction. It is permitted to say what is necessary to predispose her to the act, but not other things. R. Yochanan said: These are the words of R. Yochanan b. Dehavai, but the Sages said: "The *halacha* is not in accordance with Yochanan b. Dehavai, but whatever a man wishes to do with his wife, he may do. . . . " Amemar said: "Who are the ministering angels [cited by R. Yochanan b. Dehavai]? They are the Rabbis [of that time, who, apparently, had scaled transcendent peaks of purity]."

The point is clear. "The Torah was not given to the ministering angels," but to men of flesh and blood. And though our history has been brilliantly illuminated by some men who have so rarefied their earthly natures as to actually rise to the level of the ministering angels, it is to the *generality* of Jews that *halacha* is directed, and to *their* natures that it corresponds. This being the case, however, if one goes off the wrong end of *halacha*, he cannot plead "Nature" — he has gone to the Devil uninvited.

At one point in [*lehavdil*] Dostoyevsky's *Crime and Punishment*, Svidrigailov, probably literature's most notorious lecher, contrasts his life-style with Raskolnikov's "Superman theory," characterizing the latter as the brain-child of a sick imagination, "whereas in this [his own] vice, at least there is something permanent, founded indeed upon *nature* [italics mine] and not dependent on *fantasy*, something present in the *blood* like an ever-burning ember, forever setting one on fire and, maybe, not to be quickly extinguished, even with years." Towards the end of his blighted career, Svidrigailov worriedly gives vent to a paradoxical piece of retrospective self-revelation: "I never had a great hatred for anyone, I never particularly desired to avenge myself even, and that's a bad sign, a bad sign, a bad sign. I never liked quarreling either, and have never lost my temper — that's a bad sign too."

Why should such wonderful things be such bad signs? The answer, at this point, should be obvious. The moment of truth has descended upon Svidrigailov. His vice is *not* in his blood; for if it were, why should his blood never boil for revenge? Why should his blood never boil in hatred? Why should his blood boil only for *that*? Why? Because he *makes* it boil; because he fans the lion's flame; because he draws forth iniquity with cords of deceit — because he *puts* the country into Salem! Svidrigailov has discovered — too late — that he has gone to the Devil uninvited.

"The fault, dear Brutus [and for our purposes we may take this as signifying the brute one *makes* himself], lies not in our *stars*, but in our *selves*, that we are underlings."

10 / THE MAN

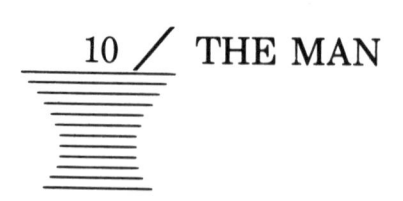

The episode of David and Bath-sheva (II *Samuel* 11-12) is a kind of microcosm of the dominant principles enunciated thus far, and it might be of value, at this point, to attempt to capture some of the light shed on that episode by the laser-beam of *chazal*:

(*Shabbath* 56a): "R. Shmuel b. Nachmani said in the name of R. Yonathan: "All who say that David sinned are mistaken."

How can they be mistaken? Did not David himself admit to Nathan the Prophet (II *Samuel* 12:13), "I have sinned against the Lord"? And did he not intone (*Psalms* 51:5), "For I know my offence, and my sin is forever before me"? The *Gemara* goes on to demonstrate that David did not sin in the gross, conventional sense of having committed murder or

* 53 * *the man*

adultery, God forbid (the details of that explanation are not our immediate concern). In what sense *did* David sin, then? The most direct way to grasp the nature of David's sin is through God's chastisement of David by the allegory that He placed in the mouth of Nathan the Prophet, and to which David responded: "I have sinned against the Lord." If it is the allegory which elicits that response, it must be the allegory itself which demonstrates to David (and to us) the nature of his sin. Let us consider the allegory, then:

(II *Samuel* 12-13): And the Lord sent Nathan to David. And he came to him and said to him: "There were two men in one city, the one rich, and the other poor. The rich man had very many flocks and herds; but the poor man had nothing except one little ewe-lamb, which he had bought and reared. And it grew up together with him and with his children. It ate of his bread, and drank of his cup, and lay in his bosom, and was like a daughter to him. And there came a wayfarer to the rich man, and he thought it a pity to take of his own flock and of his own herd to prepare it for the guest who had come to him, but he took the poor man's lamb, and prepared it for the man who came to him." And David's anger burned greatly against the man; and he said to Nathan, "As the Lord lives, the man that has done this deserves to die; and he shall restore the lamb fourfold, because he did this thing, and because he had no pity."

Then Nathan said to David, "You are the man. Thus says the Lord God of Israel: I anointed you king over Israel, and I delivered you out of the hand of Saul, and I gave you your master's house, and your master's wives into your bosom, and I gave you the house of Israel and of Judah. And if that had been too little, I would moreover have given you as much again. Why have you despised the commandment of the Lord, to do evil in His sight? You have killed Uria the Hittite with the sword and have taken his wife to be your wife, and have slain him with the sword of the children of Ammon. Now, therefore, the sword shall never depart from your house, because you have despised me and have taken the wife of Uria the Hittite to be your wife. Thus says the Lord: Behold, I will raise up evil against you out of your own house, and I will take your wives before your eyes and give them to your neighbor; and he shall lie down with your wives in the sight of this sun. For you did it secretly; but I will do this thing before all Israel, and before the sun." And David said to Nathan, "I have sinned against the Lord."

Immediately we are struck by discrepancies between the allegory and the analogue. It is obvious that the rich man is David; the poor man, Uria; the lamb, Bath-sheva. But who is this mysterious "man" for whom the rich man prepared the sheep? Did David take Bath-sheva for any other man but himself? And why should David allow himself to be so easily incriminated by the allegory? Could he not quite justifiably have countered: "How can you make such a comparison! Bath-sheva is not a 'little ewe-lamb'! She is everything! She is the sublimest of the sublime! It is

*   55   *   *the man*

not I who was the rich man, but Uria! Not Uria who was the poor man, but I! What was my master's house and my master's wives to me if I did not have Bathsheva!" Yet David did not say this. He said only, "I have sinned against the Lord." Why? Here we must stand in reverential awe at the feet of our Sages and receive their answer:

(*Sukka* 52b): R. Huna asked: In one place it is written (*Hosea* 4:11), "For the spirit of harlotry has led them astray" [implying that this "spirit" is an outer force], and in another (*ibid.* 5:4), "For the spirit of harlotry is *within* them" [implying the opposite! The answer:] In the beginning, it is an outside force, and in the end, it resides within them. Rava said: In the beginning, the *yetzer hara* is called a "wayfarer" [an *outside* force, stemming not from the demands of man's inner, essential nature, but from imaginative weavings, quite external to his true, natural needs]; then it is called a "guest" [i.e. it insinuates itself from the outside into his inner being; it begins to make itself "at home" within him]; and, finally, it is called "the man" [it becomes indistinguishable from the man himself, so that he feels and assumes not that his *yetzer hara* needs something, but that *he* needs it, that his very nature cries out for it, and that to deny it is to deny nature itself! (One of our great men once said that man's greatest task is not to confuse *himself* with his *yetzer hara*)]. This is the import of the verse (II *Samuel* 12:4): "And there came a *wayfarer* to the rich man, and he thought it a pity to take of his own flock and of his own herd, to prepare it for the *guest* . . . and he prepared it for the *man* that came to him."

The message was not lost upon David. There were no discrepancies. Allegory and analogue were terrifyingly exact. Yes, Bath-sheva was only "a little ewe-lamb." Certainly, the woman who was to be the mother of King Solomon possessed excellent qualities, even sublime qualities. But it was not *this* sublimity and *this* incomparability that David had witnessed from the roof of his palace that night when he chanced to see her bathing — although he thought it was, or — to be more exact — although he thought *he* thought it was. Nathan's allegory told David (and it told him with a power of Truth that was not be contested) that it was not *he* who had desired Bath-sheva, but his *yetzer hara*; that as far as *he* was concerned, Bath-sheva, at that moment, was only "a little ewe-lamb," and that his many wives were not one jot inferior to her in terms of what he saw *at that time*. He *was* the rich man! Uria *was* the poor man! It was not *you*, the rich man, to whom you gave Bath-sheva, but to that mysterious stranger, who had originated as a "wayfarer," mediated as a "guest," and terminated as "the man." The allegory fits — oh, too, exactly. There was only one response that one could make to such an allegory: "I have sinned against the Lord."

But at this very juncture in the *Gemara*, and seemingly from out of nowhere, an ominous chord is struck:

R. Yochanan said: There is a small organ in a man.

If he satisfies it, it goes hungry; if he lets it go hungry, it is satisfied — as it is written (*Hosea* 13:6): "When they were broken [not satisfied] they were sated; when they were satisfied, their hearts were lifted — therefore, they have forgotten Me."

What does this mean? Why is it stated here? Hasn't everything been resolved? Apparently not.

11 / "IF YOUR FOE IS HUNGRY, FEED HIM BREAD"

(*Sanhedrin* 107a): R. Yehuda said in the name of Rav: Let one never put himself to the test; for David, king of Israel, put himself to the test, and he succumbed. He questioned, "Lord of the universe, why is it stated [in the *Shemoneh Esrey*]: "God of Abraham, God of Isaac, God of Jacob," and not "God of David"? God answered, "They were tested by Me, but you were not tested by Me." At this, David said, "Lord of the universe, test me," as it is written (*Psalms* 26:2): "Prove me, O Lord, and test me." God replied, "I shall test you, and I shall even do something special for you. For I did not inform them of the nature of their tests, but I am informing you that you shall be tested in the area of lust" — whereupon (II *Samuel* 11:2): "And it was towards evening, and David arose from his bed" [after which follows the episode with Bath-sheva. But the *Gemara* is struck by something about this introduction to the episode with Bath-sheva, something, perhaps, which only a child (or a philosopher) would ever think of noticing (and which proves to be the key to *everything!*): Why is it "towards evening" that David is arising? What is the king of Israel — and such a king! — doing in bed in the daytime?] R. Yehuda explained: He had converted his bed of night to his bed of day [i.e. he cohabited with his wives during the day rather than at night, so that when the "test" came (and he assumed that this kind of test would, most likely, come at night), he would have assuaged his lust and would be invulnerable to any new enticement]. But here he had overlooked a *halacha* [and *halacha* is being used here in its literal sense of "going." A *halacha*, correctly understood, is a statement of how life "goes," how nature truly operates. *Halacha*, in its purest sense, is not a mandate from without, but a statement of what goes on within (see pages 45-47)]; and David had "overlooked" (of course, it was a *yetzer haraian* slip) the following truism of nature (prepare yourself for an old acquaintance)]: "There is a small organ in a man. If he satisfies it, it goes hungry; if he lets it go hungry, it is satisfied."

Now — in this context — it is clear: David was informed of the adversary against which he would be pitted, and he prepared for the confrontation — but his strategy backfired! Instead of steeling him for the encounter, it became a kind of encounter in itself and completely incapacitated him for the trial that was to follow. And why so? The key lies in the phrase, "a small organ." Of course, it is not physical size that is being referred to, but strength of demand; and, understood in this way, the paradox is readily resolved:

The sexual appetite is not like the appetite for food. The latter is essentially body-based, nature-based, reality-based — so that with it we would expect the normal, non-paradoxical sequence: gratification inducing satiety, and non-gratification inducing hunger. David's "error" was to reason from *this* appetite to the other. But the sexual appetite does not work this way! As a matter of fact, it works just the opposite way! And why so? Because (as it most frequently manifests itself) the sexual appetite is essentially imagination-based. Its body component is minimal — "a *small* organ." Such an appetite works in paradoxical sequence: gratification induces hunger, and non-gratification, satiety. The imagination thrives on attention. The more one preoccupies himself with it, the more it is stimulated; the less he deals with it, the less it asserts itself. And this stands to reason; for where there is a *real* appetite, then giving it what it *really* is in need of will satisfy it; but where most of the appetite is fabrication to begin with, then most of what it receives is not food at all, but additional fabrication — fabrication heaped upon fabrication!

(*Sukka* 52a): Solomon called it [the *yetzer hara*] "the foe," as it is written (*Proverbs* 25:21): "If your foe

✳ 61 ✳ *if your foe is hungry*

is hungry, feed him bread; and if he is thirsty, give him water to drink."

Is this a call to self-indulgence? Has King Solomon, God forbid, suddenly turned hedonist? By no means whatsoever. The meaning is: If your foe is hungry, feed him *only* bread — and not visionary viands; if he is thirsty, give him *only* water to drink — and not ambrosial nectar. Your bodily demands are small. They can be easily satisfied with sparse, simple, *bodily* fare.* Do not build the bodily base into a monster of

---

* In this connection, Rambam writes (*Mishneh Torah, Hilchoth De'oth* 4:19): Semen is the strength and life of the body and the light of one's eyes; and the more that is emitted, the more the body and its strength wane and its life is dissipated. As King Solomon said in his wisdom (*Proverbs* 31:3), "Do not give your strength to women." If one over-indulges in coitus, old age "leaps" upon him: his strength fades, his eyes grow dim, a foul odor issues from his mouth and his arm-pits; the hair of his head, his eye-brows, and his eye-lids drops out; the hair of his beard, his arm-pits, and his legs proliferates; his teeth fall out; and many ills, other than these, beset him. The doctors say [and the Rambam was one of the greatest doctors of his age], "One of a thousand dies of other illnesses, and the thousand from over-indulgence in coitus." Therefore, one must exercise caution in this matter if he wishes to live well. He should have intercourse only when his body is healthy and strong and he finds himself frequently hardening unwittingly and unable to relieve this hardening by turning his attention to other matters. [Here Rambam provides some additional information for ascertaining when the *body* (as opposed to the imagination) is in need of coitus.]

He writes further (*Issurey Biya* 21:11): The Sages do not look favorably upon one who over-indulges in coitus and "flutters about his wife like a rooster." His character is considered extremely defective and his conduct boorish. But one who is abstemious in

imagination; for then you will be converting a potential "foe" into an actual one.

intercourse is to be praised (provided he does not skip the prescribed conjugal times without his wife's consent.)
 (*Cautionary note:* Any resemblance between the forgeries of imagination and the holiness of the marital union is purely peripheral and coincidental, and no implications are to be drawn from one area to the other.)

12 / THE BEEHIVE

In *Sanhedrin* 107a we read: (II *Samuel* 11:2): "And he walked upon the roof of the palace, and from the roof, he saw a woman bathing; and the woman was very fair to look upon." Bath-sheva was shampooing her hair under a beehive when Satan appeared to David in the guise of a bird. He shot an arrow at the bird [but it missed] and it broke the beehive, at which she was revealed, and he saw her — whereupon (*ibid.* 3) "David sent and inquired after the woman, and he said: 'Is this not Bath-sheva, the daughter of Eliam, the wife of Uria the Hittite?' And David sent messengers, and took her; and she came in to him, and he lay with her."

The above allegory follows immediately upon the revelation of David's "strategy," and is, accordingly, to be understood as mirroring its consequences. Again, let us ask some good children's questions: A beehive is such a small thing; how can it hide a person? If "she was revealed," then certainly he "saw her." Or, as we would ask in our sublime sophistication: "Why the redundancy?" At this point, we *know* the answers; it only remains for us to place them in their proper slots:

The beehive is the ungratified *yetzer hara*, housing a big potential "sting" (if it is gratified). The beehive "hides" Bath-sheva as an object of desire; for when the *yetzer hara* is ungratified, it is sated. The *Gemara* itself helps us with the bird, telling us that it is Satan, God's messenger, whose job it is to overwhelm us with the *yetzer hara*. David's shooting the arrow at the bird is obviously his attempt to kill the *yetzer hara*. And we already know what the arrow is. It is his strategy of "gratify and satisfy." But we already know, too, that this strategy is going to backfire, that it will do the very opposite of what it was intended to do. The arrow, by missing Satan and breaking open the beehive of ungratified desire, will release the giant sting that was lurking there all the time. Bath-sheva will be "revealed," not as the ewe-lamb that she is, but as an object of immense desire; David will "see her" with eyes of lust — and he will fail the test.

David, however, was not one to fail a test without growing from his failure. Once it had been impressed upon him that "Imagination" was the name of the villain, not only did he learn to subdue it, but he eventually gained such mastery over it as to actually *exploit* it!

✱ 65 ✱ *the beehive*

Many have wondered about the necessity for the inclusion of the "unsavory" episode of Avishag the Shunamite in Scripture. After all, what constructive, edifying purpose is served by telling us that when David was old he was not warm and Avishag the Shunamite was selected as the most beautiful virgin in all of Israel (I *Kings* 1:4): "And the maiden was extremely beautiful, and kept the king warm, and she served him, and the king did not cohabit with her." Why tell us this?

Again, let us ask a child's question: If the only purpose in all this was to keep the king warm, why must it be only the most beautiful woman in all of Israel who can serve this purpose? Or (to be more sophisticated again), since when is there a positive correlation between beauty and heat? And if her beauty can excite him to warmth, how can it not excite him to conjugal intimacy with her — unless we say that he was so old that he *could* not be excited to cohabitation — in which case, how could her beauty excite him to warmth? These questions are not "beneath" the *Gemara* itself. They are of paramount importance:

(*Sanhedrin* 22a): "Avishag said to David, 'Marry me.' He answered, 'You are forbidden to me' [he already had his permissible 'quota' of eighteen wives]. At this, she said to him: 'When the thief cannot find what to steal, he parades himself as a paragon of virtue' [i.e. your age has deprived you of your virility]." At this point the *Gemara* goes on to indicate how David demonstrated (within the bounds of morality) that this was far from being the case.

What is happening here? What is happening is a miracle of self-control, the harnessing by a mortal of the powers of his imagination to the extent that it is converted from the arch-enemy of his being to its staunchest ally, to the extent that it becomes a purely functional instrument, so delicately attuned by its possessor as to supply only needed warmth, but prevented from rising the additional "degrees" that would render it corruptive heat. David had reached that mind-boggling level where his imagination could convert Avishag's great beauty to warmth and not lust! If one who *subdues* his *yetzer hara* is a hero (*Avoth* 4:1), how much more so one who *harnesses* it!

Who but a David could do this? Who but David, king of Israel, could enter the beehive itself and emerge triumphantly with the honey — without the sting!

13 / WHAT IS TZNIUTH?

If the *yetzer hara* was born in Eden, so was *tzniuth* (loosely rendered "modesty"), and it is back to Eden that we must go to trace it to its roots.

(*Genesis* 2:25): "And they were both naked, the man and his wife, and they were not ashamed." Rashi: "For they did not know the way of *tzniuth,* to differentiate between good and evil. And even though Adam had been given knowledge to give names to the animals, he was not given a *yetzer hara* until he ate from the Tree of Knowledge and a *yetzer hara* entered into him, and he knew the difference between good and evil."

Rashi immediately upsets our traditional concepts by indicating to us that *tzniuth* does not mean covering oneself. (Let it be said immediately that covering oneself is, of course, an implication or extension of the idea of *tzniuth*; but it is not the *meaning* of *tzniuth*.) *Tzniuth*, rather, is an ability — the ability "to differentiate between good and evil." But just when we think we are understanding things perfectly, Rashi unleashes as exasperating a *non sequitur* as one might hope to encounter anywhere: "And even though Adam had been given knowledge to give names to the animals, he was not given a *yetzer hara* until he ate from the Tree of Knowledge." How did the animals suddenly come into this? And now that they are here, what kind of "even though" is this? "*Even though* he could name animals, he did not have a *yetzer hara*!" (And, if we had not had the good fortune of alighting upon Rambam [see "The *Yetzer Hara*," pages 12 - 16] our biggest question would be addressed to Rashi's paradox: "A *yetzer hara* entered into him, and he knew the difference between good and evil"! According to Rashi [but now we know why] the lowly *yetzer hara* is a prerequisite for the sublime knowledge of good and evil!) What, however, does all this have to do with *tzniuth*?

To answer these questions, we must go back to the naming of the animals — and even before that (*Genesis* 2:18): "And the Lord God said: It is not good that man be alone; I shall make him a helpmate." Immediately thereafter: "And the Lord God formed out of the ground every beast of the field and every fowl of heaven, and brought them to the man to see what he would call them; and all that the man called every living creature, that is its name." It is clear, then, that the naming of the animals is going to have something to do with providing a helpmate for Adam. But what? And how are we to understand "and all that the man called every living creature, that is its name"? Naturally, if he called a creature thus-and-so, then that is its name.

The matter is to be understood thus: "One who gives a gift to his neighbor must inform him that he is doing so" (so that the receiver will feel gratitude to the giver). God was about to give man his greatest gift. To ensure Adam's recognition of the great value of this gift, He would place him in a situation which would impress upon him his incompleteness, the void that existed in his nature, so that when Eve was conferred upon him, he would see her as filling that tremendous void, would be that much more cognizant of the greatness of the gift, and that much more grateful to the Giver. That situation was the naming of the animals.

Hebrew is called *lashon hakodesh* (the "holy language"). This is not a mere, empty phrase. It is to be taken quite literally. Hebrew (unlike other languages, which are merely sets of arbitrary symbols for the labeling of things) is a *holy* language; it does not label things, but *characterizes* them. In other languages, the word *names* the thing; in *lashon hakodesh*, it *is* the thing, the very distillation of its essence. So that when God instructed Adam to name the animals, He was not asking him to label them, but to identify them. And

Adam, at that time, was capable of such identification because he had not yet eaten from the Tree of Knowledge and possessed not the inferior "good-bad" variety of intellect, but the Godly, "true-false" variety. In short, in naming the animals, Adam was penetrating into their very natures — and finding that they did not correspond to his! Every creature possessed a mate whose nature complemented its own, but he, Adam, did not! He saw — and he saw with the eyes of intense, unerring *truth* — that there was a tremendous void within him crying out to be filled! "And all that the man called every living creature, that is its name" — that is its *real* name — not a mere label, but an epitomization! It is not surprising, then, that immediately after the foregoing verse we read (*ibid.* 20): "And the man gave names to all the cattle and to the fowl of the air, and to every beast of the field; but he did not find a helpmate for Adam." The tone itself spills forth the meaning: "He did not find a helpmate for *Adam*, although he had found one for all other creatures." And it is only at this juncture that God performs His revolutionary operation, awakening from which, Adam cries out in an ecstasy of recognition (*ibid.* 23): "*This* time [as opposed to the other times in the naming process, when I searched in vain for my counterpart, I find] bone of *my* bone, and flesh of *my* flesh. [Only] *this* one shall be called *isha* because [only] she was taken from *ish*." Rashi here adduces the terse summation of the Sages (*Yevamoth* 63a): "This teaches us that Adam cohabited with every beast and

what is tzniuth?

animal, but was not fulfilled until he lived with Eve." This is obviously not be understood in its literal sense (which would pose a *physical* impossibility), but in terms of what has just been stated. Adam was "intimate" with every beast and animal (the term *vayeyda* "and he knew," for example, can connote either cognitive or sexual intimacy). He penetrated into the very core of their natures, and the truth in him testified: "This is not me!" It is only Eve that struck the responsive chord, only Eve who fulfilled him, only Eve about whom it could truly be said: "*She* was taken from man." God's structured "situation" had come full cycle. He had given the gift, and it had been duly recognized.

We are now prepared to return to our starting point (*Genesis* 2:25): "And they were both naked, the man and his wife, and were not ashamed." Rashi: "For they did not know the way of *tzniuth*, to differentiate between good and evil. And *even though* Adam had been given knowledge to give names to the animals [so that one might ask: "If he had the mind to be able to penetrate into the very nature of the animals and verbally crystallize their very essence, then why at that time did he not possess *tzniuth*, the ability to differentiate between good and evil?" — if one would ask this question, the answer is], he was not given a *yetzer hara* until he ate from the Tree of Knowledge and a *yetzer hara* entered into him and [it was only through the *deception* of the *yetzer hara* that] he knew the difference between good and evil"! The paradox is the point! Relative to man's prior knowledge, the knowledge of good and evil is not good, but bad, a figment of the *yetzer hara*. And — paradox of paradoxes — it is only the *yetzer hara* which produces *tzniuth*, the recognition of a good-evil (as opposed to a true-false) situation!

Tzniuth, then, does not mean covering oneself. It does mean recognizing a "bad" situation, which dictates that one cover himself. (Before the *yetzer hara*, that "bad" situation would have been a "neutral" one, which would have dictated no covering whatsoever.)

The following, concerning the public humiliation of a *sota* (a woman accused of infidelity) is a case in point:

(*Sota* 7a): *Mishna*: . . . The *kohein* seizes her garment. If it tears, it tears; and if it is rent [a larger tear], it is rent — until he uncovers her breast; and he unbinds her hair. R. Yehuda said: "If her breast was fair, he did not expose it; and if her hair was fair, he did not unbind it."

Gemara: This would seem to indicate that Rabbi Yehuda is apprehensive of lewd thoughts [on the part of the onlookers, if she would be thus exposed], and the Rabbis [who permit such exposure] are not. But did we not learn just the opposite, viz.: "A man who is to be stoned [by the *beth din*] is covered in one section, in front [his genitals — he is left otherwise naked, so that his agony will not be prolonged — even for a fraction of a second — by the buffer of clothing], and a woman is covered in two sections, in front and in back, because her genital region is partially visible from the back."

what is tzniuth?

These are the words of R. Yehuda [which would seem to indicate that he is *not* apprehensive of lewd thoughts on the part of the onlookers; for aside from these two regions, she is entirely uncovered.] And the Rabbis say: "A man is stoned naked [except for that one region], but a woman is not stoned naked" [she must be fully clothed — which would seem to indicate that the Rabbis *are* apprehensive of lewd thoughts on the part of the onlookers — in direct contradiction to what is stated by the *Mishna*!] Rabba answered [that R. Yehuda does not contradict himself: Why is it that a *sota* is not to be subjected to the aforementioned exposure?] "For there is a possibility that she may leave the *beth din* vindicated [and not be killed] and remain a perpetual source of enticement to the young *kohanim* [who had witnessed her exposure]. But in the case of stoning, she is gone!" And if you ask: "But will the fact that he witnessed her naked before her *execution* not cause other women to be enticing to him?" In this connection, Rava stated: "We have learned that the *yetzer hara* entices one only in respect of what his eyes gaze at [and does not transfer from her to a different object] . . ."

Now what happens to the laws of *tzniuth* in all of this? And if we knew for a certainty that she would not leave the *beth din* vindicated, why would it then be unquestionably permissible to expose her thus? And why is it permitted to behold an unclothed woman being stoned? Is she not still a woman?

The answer: When one beholds a woman who is

going to die, imagination does not invest her with romance, and she is seen correctly (not within the good-bad gestalt, but within the true-false gestalt) as skin, blood, and bones. This, then, is not a *yetzer hara* situation; and any situation which is not a *yetzer hara* situation is, by definition, not a *tzniuth* situation. Why cover what is already a covering — and *only* a covering!

And as to that great principle that we have received through tradition — "The *yetzer hara* entices one only in respect of what his eyes gaze at" — is it not clear why it should, indeed, be so? — why the *same* arousal induced by one object should not be transferable to another object of the same kind? It should be clear. It is not the "kind," primarily, which produces the arousal, but the imagination; and the *distinct* images that the imagination places in one configuration, it will not place in a different configuration — though they be configurations of the same "kind"!

Another instance (*Berachoth* 20a): R. Gidel would sit at the door of the ritualarium and instruct the women: "Immerse yourself thus; immerse yourself thus." The Rabbis asked him: "Has the master no fear of the *yetzer hara*?" He answered: "In my eyes, they are like a flock of white geese."

A violation of the laws of *tzniuth*? Certainly not; an instance, rather, where a *tzniuth* situation does not exist. Where the *yetzer hara* does not exist, *tzniuth* does not exist; and R. Gidel was telling the Rabbis that he was not seeing things through the eyes of the *yetzer hara*, that he was seeing not a "bad" situation, but a

what is tzniuth?

"neutral" one. (It is to be noted from their very question that the Rabbis themselves, great as they were, were not seeing things that way.)

And yet another instance (*Kethuboth* 17a): R. Acha would carry the bride on his shoulders and dance with her. The Rabbis asked him: "May we do the same thing?" He answered: "If she is to you as a beam of wood [as she is to me], then, by all means, you may do so; but if not, you may not." [It is not recorded that any of the Rabbis took him up on this proposal.]

Was R. Acha placing himself "above the law"? Certainly not; he was simply identifying something as a non-legalistic situation (for himself). *Once* there were such men.

And the truth is that we need not resort to such extravagant exceptions to the norm to bear out the point. Are doctors "above" the laws of *tzniuth*? Are their patients above these laws? What happens to the laws of *tzniuth*, for example, when a woman walks into an obstetrician's office? Are they conveniently discarded? God forbid. What the doctor sees [or is adjudged capable of seeing] in his practice is not an imagination-ridden *yetzer hara* situation, but a neutral one, a clinical one [or as our Sages express it: "He is engaged in his occupation"]. That same doctor, and that same patient, however, the moment they walk out of that office, are transported as it were, into a different world, a different gestalt. They are transported back into a *yetzer hara* situation, and all the laws of *tzniuth* which the moment before did not *apply* [it would be inaccurate to say that they had been *rescinded*] now *do apply*. This is not situational ethics. It is not that some situations *override* the laws of *tzniuth*, but that some situations, by their very nature, are not *yetzer hara* situations, and, therefore, not *tzniuth* situations.

The root of "*tzniuth*" actually appears only twice in all of Scripture — once in *Micha* (6:8): "He has told you, O man, what is good; and what does the Lord require of you, but to do justly, and to love lovingkindness, and to walk with *tzniuth* [*vehatznea lecheth* — generally translated 'and to walk humbly'] with your God"; and again in *Proverbs* (11:2): "When pride comes, then comes shame; but with *tznuim* [generally translated 'the lowly'] is wisdom." It is instructive to note that in neither of these instances does *tzniuth* appear within the context of covering, but, oddly enough, within that of false weights and measures! The verse in *Micha* is followed thus (6:9-11): "The Lord's voice cries to the city, and the man of wisdom shall see Your name; hear the rod and who has appointed it. Are there yet the treasures of wickedness in the house of the wicked, and the scant measure that is abominable? Shall I count myself pure with wicked balances, and with a bag of deceitful weights?" And the verse preceding that in *Proverbs* (indeed, the very chapter introduction) is (11:1): "A false balance is abomination to the Lord; but a just weight is His delight." Nothing whatsoever about covering.

The explanation, in view of what has gone before, is

what is tzniuth?

not hard to find. *Tzniuth*, in its elemental sense, denotes the recognition of a good-bad situation. Indeed, it is only within this framework that we can at all understand the verse in *Micha*: "What does the Lord require of you, but to do justly and to love lovingkindness, and to walk with *tzniuth*." Indeed! What more *could* He require of us? Is this a small order? It is everything!

The clue to the answer lies in the preceding verse (7): "Shall I give my first-born for my transgression, the fruit of my body for the sin of my soul?" — immediately followed by: "He has told you, O man, what is good; and what does the Lord require of you," etc. In context, it is abundantly clear: "Does the Lord want 'the fruit of your body'? Does He expect you to tear yourself apart? Does He expect anything *unnatural* from you? He has told you what is *good*. *All* He expects of you is *good*. He expects nothing more exalted from you than doing justly and loving lovingkindness — in short, nothing *more* than walking with *tzniuth*, in accordance with the recognition of good and evil, something which your nature is, and should be capable of. He is not holding you to the unnatural, unattainable standard of true-false recognition. Is He, then, asking too much?

And what is a more basic, more elemental, more tangible embodiment of a "bad" situation than false weights and measures? Indeed, what can better serve as a *symbol* for such a situation?

We are not expected to be ministering angels, but

only to be honest to the natural resources within us — and there are resources of *tzniuth* within our natures.

"And walk with *tzniuth* with your God."

14 / AFTERWORD

"The Torah was not given to the ministering angels." "Who are the ministering angels? — the Rabbis." There is no contradiction here, but only an expression of the difference between what human nature is and what it is within its province to become. This is not to say that we can realistically expect to reach the heights of those giants of old (this would be the height of pretension and obtuseness on our part); it *is* to say, however, that such heights do exist within the *theoretical* possibilities of our nature, and that if we cannot *reach* them, at least we can *aspire* to them. Aspiration in itself is elevating. If it does not get us where we want to go, at least it gets us a little farther than we are now. As a wise man once put it: "The mariners do not expect to reach the stars, but they use them to steer by."

We may well have to face the fact that we shall never get the country out of Salem; but if we can divest it of a waterfall or two, or even dilute to some extent some of the springtime fragrance that pervades it, we will have come a long way in our battle with the *yetzer hara*. We will have come that much closer to *truth* and to the eternal Universal Truth that is God.